LET YOUR VOICE BE HEARD

LET YOUR VOICE BE HEARD

THE LIFE AND TIMES OF Pete Seeger

ANITA SILVEY

Clarion Books

HOUGHTON MIFFLIN HARCOURT

BOSTON NEW YORK

Clarion Books

3 Park Avenue

New York, New York 10016

Copyright © 2016 by Anita Silvey

Clarion Books is an imprint of Houghton Mifflin Harcourt Publishing Company.

www.hmhco.com

The text was set in Freight Text.

Design by Lisa Vega

Library of Congress Cataloging-in-Publication Data

Silvey, Anita.

Let your voice be heard : the life and times of Pete Seeger / Anita Silvey.

pages cm

Includes bibliographical references and index.

ISBN 978-0-547-33012-9 (hardcover)

1. Seeger, Pete, 1919-2014—Juvenile literature.

2. Folk singers—United States—Biography—Juvenile literature. I. Title.

ML3930.S42S55 2016

782.42162'130092—dc23

[B]

2015034787

Manufactured in the United States of America

DOC 10 9 8 7 6 5 4 3 2 1

4500605140

For Vicki and Steve Palmquist,

for all they have done for me and so many others

CONTENTS

INTRODUCTION . . . 1

THE BEGINNINGS . . . 3

MENTORS AND SCHOOL . . . 10

CHOOSING MUSIC . . . 18

BECOMING A PERFORMER . . . 25

SUCCESS AT LAST . . . 37

UNDER SUSPICION . . . 45

FIGHTING BACK . . . 53

JOINING FORCES . . . 64

SINGING TOGETHER TO SAVE
OUR PLANET . . . 73

PETE SEEGER'S LEGACY . . . 81

AFTERWORD . . . 87

SOURCE NOTES . . . 89

BIBLIOGRAPHY . . . 96

PHOTO CREDITS . . . 99

ACKNOWLEDGMENTS . . . 100

INDEX . . . 102

INTRODUCTION

In 1949 banjo player Pete Seeger drove to Peekskill, New York, to perform in a concert featuring the great singer Paul Robeson. The first attempt at this event had been canceled. Because Robeson was African American, a local branch of the American Legion had destroyed the stage and equipment and had assaulted some of the young people preparing for the concert.

A week later the performers tried again. Seeger vividly recalled what happened that night.

When the concert was over, we all congratulated ourselves that things had gone smoothly. But the cars seemed to leave very slowly. When our car—a station wagon, carrying my wife, two babies, their grandfather, and two friends—pulled out of the gate, the policeman would not let us turn left or go straight ahead. He directed all traffic down one narrow road. . . .

Suddenly we saw a lot of broken glass on the road . . .

Up ahead were young men with piles of fist-sized stones heaving them at every car that passed. . . . Only a hundred feet away was a policeman.

"Officer, aren't you going to do something about this?"

"Move on! Keep moving!" he shouted angrily. . . .

In the next two miles ten or fifteen rocks hit us. Every window in the car was broken.

Eventually Pete and his family got back home, covered in shards of glass. Later he cemented into his fireplace three of the stones that had come into the car that night. He never wanted to forget this incident when people had tried to stop him from singing.

THE BEGINNINGS

Oh Shenandoah, I long to hear you,
Away you rolling river,
Oh Shenandoah, I long to hear you,
Away I'm bound away
'Cross the wide Missouri.
(Traditional ballad)

Pete Seeger became the most important folk singer of the twentieth and twenty-first centuries. But he might have chosen a very different path. Although his grandfather made a fortune from sugar refining in Mexico, Pete became an advocate for underpaid workers. Though he came from financial privilege, he identified with those who had to make a living. He fought for the oppressed and poor all his life.

Pete Seeger was descended from a long line of Americans, many of whom had held prominent positions in society. His earliest American ancestors sailed from England on the *Mayflower* in 1620. Some of their descendants fought on the Patriots' side in the American Revolution. At the Battle of Bunker Hill, one of Pete's relatives walked down the hill backwards because he didn't want to turn his back and run from the British. Family members who came later became abolitionists, fighting to free the slaves. "Other relatives experimented with Christian Science, yogism, nudism, advocated women's suffrage, pacifism, vegetarianism, organic gardening. . . . This might all add up to sound like a family full of crackpots."

Pete's parents were highly educated, economically privileged, and very talented. His father, Charles Seeger Jr., had grown up in a house where he was waited on by servants. Pete's mother, Constance de Clyver Edson, a violinist, and his father were both classical musicians. Charles studied music at Harvard. Constance trained at the Paris Conservatory. In 1911 Charles Seeger and Constance left New England so that Charles could join the faculty at the University of California in Berkeley as the youngest full professor in the history of the school.

In California's San Joaquin Valley, Charles came into contact with scores of agricultural migrant workers. Nothing in his upbringing had prepared him for the terrible conditions in which these people lived—in makeshift tents, with crude bathroom facilities. His exposure to their misery changed the way he viewed the world. At the age of six, children who looked like his sons, Charles and John, were being worked like slaves. Charles was appalled.

Soon he began visiting the offices of the Industrial Workers of the World (the IWW, known as the Wobblies) in San Francisco. Labor leader Eugene Debs had founded the organization in 1905 with the goal of unionizing all workers. They believed that peace would never exist as long as workers faced hunger and poverty. Charles supported their goals and started distributing IWW leaflets to migrant workers when he wasn't teaching.

After the United States entered the Great War (later known as World War I) in 1917, Charles was required to register as a soldier in California. He declared himself a conscientious objector (CO), unable to serve because he opposed the war. This was a risky step, because draft boards across the country were jailing COs and labeling them "traitors." Charles's older brother, Alan, on the other hand, couldn't wait to go to war. Alan wrote a poem containing the often-quoted line "I have a

Pete's father, Charles Louis Seeger, became an early advocate for the rights of workers. He was Pete's first and most influential mentor.

rendezvous with death." Later, Alan was mowed down by machine-gun fire. Charles had no intention of fighting. The judge taking a statement for the draft board suggested that Charles give up his attempt to be a conscientious objector; he was so underweight that the army would be unlikely to draft him anyway. Charles refused to do things the easy way. When he was ordered to report to a military camp in September 1918, Charles, Constance, and their sons fled California to avoid the army and relocated on the Seeger estate in Patterson, New York, sixty miles north of New York City. Peter Seeger was born on May 3, 1919.

Instead of fighting, Charles decided he wanted to perform classical music for those living in rural areas of America and introduce them to its pleasures. Shortly after Pete's birth, Charles built a trailer to pull behind a Model T Ford and headed south with his family. The trailer even carried a folding pump organ.

They traveled slowly, very slowly, over unpaved roads. Pete's older brothers had small bunks; Pete's cradle hung from hoops in the canvas roof of the trailer. When they stopped, Constance boiled diapers in an iron pot over an open fire.

The Seegers quickly learned that local people didn't want to hear classical music. They had their own music, sung and played on fiddles and banjos. Although the Seegers didn't create a classical music audience in Appalachia, they exposed their sons to the sound of Appalachian music. Pete Seeger heard his first authentic folk music as a baby.

The Seeger family caravan. Pete's mother, a violinist, holds Pete's hand; his father and brothers John and Charles are in the car.

Traveling around the country with three young children proved to be a great strain for Constance. One night she pulled Pete, a baby with long silky-blond hair and blue eyes, from the embers of their campfire. She had had enough. After a few months on the road, she insisted that they return to the family estate in New York.

Tensions between Pete's mother and father continued after the Appalachian trip. Although the couple struggled to make their marriage

Pete and his father, mother, and brothers in Washington, D.C., 1921. Pete's father is playing their portable pump organ.

work, eventually they separated and then divorced in 1927, when Pete was eight years old. The children were told nothing about what their parents were doing, and Pete was confused. At one point he said to his father, "We're having such a nice time—where's mother?"

But Pete's life changed with his parents' divorce. From third grade on he was sent away to boarding schools, spending little time with either parent. Usually he had contact with his family only during holidays and summers. Rather than growing up in a close, stable family that he could depend on for what he needed, Pete had to become self-sufficient and find mentors who could help him find his way.

~2~
MENTORS AND SCHOOL

Once upon a time there was a little boy,
who played the ukulele.
Around town he'd go, Clink, clunk, clonk, clink, clunk!
The grown-ups would say,
"Take that thing out of here!"
(Pete Seeger, *Abiyoyo*)

To find the support and direction he needed as a child, Pete Seeger became a voracious reader, searching for information in books. After seeing what titles Pete checked out in the Nyack, New York, public library, a librarian suggested that Pete pick up the novels of Ernest Thompson Seton. Pete began to devour Seton's writings. Seton believed that if young people wanted role models, they did not need to look to Europe for heroes. Seton thought that Native Americans were remarkable for their selflessness, dignity, and morality. In Native American cultures, Seton wrote, if there was food, everybody shared; if there was no food, everybody, including the chief and his family, went hungry. The idea of communal property and sharing appealed greatly to the young Pete Seeger.

Pete paid homage to Native Americans in his own fashion:

A librarian in Nyack, New York, introduced Pete to the books of Ernest Thompson Seton. One of the founders of the Boy Scouts of America, Seton encouraged Americans to look to Native people for inspiration.

"I saved my nickels and bought myself enough unbleached muslin to build a teepee, twelve by twenty-four feet in size. I pegged it out, hemmed it up, and laced up the front. I set this out in my grandparents' cow pasture and had to install a fence around it so the cows didn't break it down. Slept in it overnight, using spruce branches for a bed. Learned to cook my food in it on a tiny fire. Later I took my teepee to school and put it in another pasture, introducing others to the idea of outdoor life.

Living outdoors provided a better education for me than any school or university."

Along with what Pete read, his father, Charles, played a major role in the development of Pete's political and ethical ideas. When Pete was thirteen, Charles married Ruth Crawford, a composer, and they had four children, Mike, Peggy, Barbara, and Penelope (Penny), who became Pete's half brother and sisters. Although Pete didn't get to see his father frequently, on occasion the young boy would visit him in New York City. Charles used their time together to pass along his own political ideas to his son. To show Pete how much of the world lived, Charles walked with him through New York's poverty-stricken Lower East Side. Buildings stood empty; the streets were poorly lit. Charles and Pete walked around until Pete's feet ached. Seeing the garbage-infested alleys, Pete realized that life could be very difficult for those without financial resources— just as his father had done in the San Joaquin Valley.

In 1932 Pete entered a private high school, one that he loved. Avon Old Farms, near Hartford, Connecticut, had a small student body of ninety. Pete didn't care much for the school uniform—fancy suit, starched shirt, bow tie, and patent leather shoes, which he hated most of all. But until he attended Avon, Pete had been fascinated with the ukulele, a four-string instrument played by strumming. Although Pete's mother wanted her son to play only classical music on the piano or violin, Pete preferred making rhythmic music on instruments like the pennywhistle

A contemporary photo of the exterior of one of the buildings in Avon Old Farms in Connecticut, Pete's favorite school.

and accordion. Finally, when Pete reached the age of eight, his mother relented and let him purchase a ukulele. At Avon he discovered a teacher who played the banjo, another instrument with four strings played by strumming.

Originally brought to America by African slaves, this instrument slowly became part of popular culture. According to Pete, "The banjo . . . was popularized in the 1830s and 1840s. It swept America, just like rock and roll did a hundred years later. Good musicians were very much distressed. They said 'How can you have good music with all that plinking and plunking going on?'" Pete liked all that plinking and plunking. He agreed with the sentiments of writer Mark Twain: "Give me the banjo. When you want genuine music . . . just smash your piano, and invoke the glory-beaming banjo."

Besides discovering the banjo at Avon, Pete realized just how much

By the Civil War, the banjo had become a popular instrument. Here a Union soldier poses with his banjo.

he liked journalism. He started a school newspaper, the *Avon Weekly Newsletter*, and loved "typing, writing, editing, cartooning, and learning how to walk up to a stranger and try to ask the right questions." On one memorable occasion one of his articles got him into trouble with the school administration. They forced him to cancel a piece about a pet Texas bull snake—owned by another student, the son of the famous poet Archibald MacLeish—that had gotten loose in one of the school buildings. Administrators feared bad publicity to the school. Pete hated himself afterward for backing down on this issue and vowed that next time he believed himself right, he would not compromise.

While still a student at Avon, in 1935, when Pete was sixteen, he discovered another passion. Traveling with his father to see and hear folk music being performed at the Ninth Annual Folk Song and Dance Festival in Asheville, North Carolina, Pete saw a five-string banjo for the first time and couldn't wait to play one. Although it would be more difficult to master than his four-string model, Pete wanted to learn how.

Pete became intrigued by folk music. "These songs had all the meat of human life in them," he remembered. "They sang of heroes, outlaws, murderers, fools. . . . Above all, they seemed frank, straightforward, honest." Pete loved the directness of the emotions conveyed in folk music —the heartbreak and despair, the love and sense of community, and the protest against injustice.

Experts disagree over what constitutes a folk song. Some say a folk song has to be old. But not Pete. He believed that folk songs are the songs that people—folk—sing. He often quoted blues singer Big Bill Broonzy, who claimed that one of his own songs had to be a folk song because "I never heard horses sing it."

But at this point in Pete's life, folk music didn't seem like it could be a career choice. He decided that he wanted to be a journalist, because he had loved newspaper work in high school. In 1936, following his older brother John and his father, Pete entered Harvard on a partial scholarship. Unfortunately, at Harvard he discovered that there was no journalism department, so he majored in sociology—but those classes bored him. By his sophomore year he acknowledged that the school wasn't a good fit—the professors seemed pompous, and the readings were of no personal use to him. Harvard wasn't impressed with Pete, either, and put him on academic probation.

Pete left Harvard in April 1938, one of the most famous dropouts from a class that included a future president of the United States, John F. Kennedy. Others who left Harvard before graduation include the writer and philosopher Henry David Thoreau; Mark Zuckerberg, founder of Facebook; Bill Gates, founder of Microsoft; and actor Matt Damon.

Pete Seeger was not destined to learn his life lessons in the ivy-covered halls of Harvard. He didn't really know what he wanted to do when he grew up, but he resisted what others expected of him. To become his own person, he had to reject his mother's idea that he should be a classical musician; he also didn't want to take the path of other boys educated in exclusive private schools. Eighteen and needing to find a job, Pete Seeger still had to figure out what work made sense for him.

~ 3 ~

CHOOSING MUSIC

Lost my partner, what'll I do?
Lost my partner, what'll I do?
Lost my partner, what'll I do?
Skip to my Lou, my darling.
(Traditional song)

Pete Seeger possessed endless enthusiasm for many different things. He loved painting, particularly watercolors. He played the ukulele and the banjo. And he loved to write. His problem would be focus. What should he choose as a way to spend his life, when so many things interested him? He even considered becoming a farmer or a forest ranger.

Six feet tall and scrawny, with a bulging Adam's apple, Pete went to New York City with some big dreams about finding work as a reporter. But securing that type of job in 1938—during a worldwide economic depression, when 19 percent of the American population was out of work—proved difficult, even impossible. So the exuberant Seeger decided to see if he could make a living as an artist. Setting out on a bicycle, he traveled across New York State. He went from one farm to another, painting a watercolor portrait of each dwelling. Then he'd offer the owners his priceless vision of their property if they would put him up overnight. After a couple of months of this, Pete returned, penniless and even thinner than before, to the city—a young man in search of direction.

Hoping to pursue his interest in watercolors, Pete took classes at the American Artists School. He was enthusiastic about his skills. Others were less so. One day in a painting class, his teacher asked him if he had any other talents.

"I play the banjo," Seeger responded cheerily.

"I've never heard you play the banjo," the instructor said, "but I'd suggest you stick to that."

At that time Pete's aunt Elizabeth Seeger taught at the Dalton School, a private school in New York. One day she asked him to sing some of his songs and offered him five dollars to play. This led to engagements at other places—schools and summer camps where he sang folk songs such as "Skip to My Lou" and "John Henry." At last he knew where he belonged. "I started to paint because I failed to get a job as a journalist. I started singing and playing more because I failed as a painter," Pete wrote.

Even out of school Pete continued to find suitable mentors and learn from them. While in New York he met another one, Alan Lomax, a larger-than-life Texan with a strong ego and a single-minded sense of purpose. A few years older than Pete, Alan worked as the assistant in

Alan Lomax playing a guitar at a music festival. Alan hired Pete to work at the Library of Congress, cataloguing music.

charge of the Archive of American Folk Song at the Library of Congress and was obsessed with bringing folk music and its message to the widest possible audience. At seventeen Alan had helped his father, John, record more than ten thousand songs in prisons in the Deep South. Alan believed that folk music—not written down but passed from one singer to another—contained the real memories and experiences of the human race. He also insisted that poor people had a culture, just as important as that of the rich and literate.

While in New York, Alan introduced Pete to folk singers who came through the city. Among them was Huddie Ledbetter, who called himself "Lead Belly." Also known as "King of the Twelve-String Guitar," Lead Belly was a compact man who moved with the grace of an athlete. An African American musician who had had a tough, violent life, he had often been in trouble with the law and had served time in prison. Lead Belly captivated Pete with his soulful renditions of songs

Lead Belly, one of Pete's important mentors, had served time in prison. But the gentle man shown with his wife, Martha, in this photograph was the one Pete met in New York.

like "Goodnight, Irene," "Old Cotton Fields at Home," and "Midnight Special."

In fall 1939 Alan Lomax offered Pete Seeger a real job with weekly pay. He invited Seeger to come work at the Archive of American Folk Song at the Library of Congress in Washington, D.C., as an assistant earning fifteen dollars a week. For young Pete Seeger it was an ear-opening apprenticeship.

At the library Pete listened to stacks of dusty phonograph records, decided which contained valuable material, and catalogued them. Day after day he listened to "instrumental and vocal music, secular and religious, of many regions, races, and languages, from Latin America as well as the U.S.A." In the process Pete acquired an encyclopedic repertoire of folk songs—the songs of "cowboys and lumberjacks, coal miners and prisoners on Southern chain gangs."

In March 1940, at a fundraising concert for migrant workers, Pete met the next mentor who would profoundly change his life. Pete marveled at the composure of the star of the show, guitar player Woody Guthrie. Seven years older than Pete, the singer from Oklahoma "ambled out, offhand and casual . . . spinning out stories and singing songs he'd made up." Woody had had a much harder life than Pete. During his childhood, his mother was placed in an asylum; his sister was burned to death in an explosion; and his father went bankrupt. Woody knew about

Woody Guthrie displays his guitar. The sticker reads: "This Machine Kills Fascists."

hard luck and hard times and could put deep feeling into the lyrics of plaintive folk songs.

When Alan Lomax invited Woody to come down to the Library of Congress and record songs, Woody and Pete found that they liked to sing together. Pete provided the banjo accompaniment Woody wanted, direct and not too fancy.

Pete had learned an immense collection of songs. But knowing songs is different from performing them. Woody Guthrie stepped in to provide the next link in Pete's education as a singer. He invited Pete, who had rarely gone west of New York's Hudson River, to travel with him around Oklahoma and Texas. It would be a life-changing trip for young Pete Seeger.

～ 4 ～
BECOMING A PERFORMER

Where are the flowers? The girls have plucked them.
Where are the girls? They've all taken husbands.
Where are the men? They're all in the army.
(From *And Quiet Flows the Don* by Mikhail Sholokhov,
inspiration for the song
"Where Have All the Flowers Gone?")

At the age of twenty-one Pete Seeger set out on a road trip with one of the greatest singers of his time—or of any time. They seemed a mismatched pair. Pete was tall, Woody short. They had radically different approaches to life. Pete didn't flirt with women; he didn't drink or smoke. Woody loved women and wine. Pete seemed as if he lived in the clouds and was made of air; Woody burned with fire. Woody seemed old and hard; Woody thought Pete was the youngest man he had ever known.

Though Woody and Pete both believed in the power of song, they had different strengths as singers. Woody's voice had a straight, clear sound. He would land on a note and sustain it, producing an almost hypnotic effect. Pete's strength was not his voice but his interpretation. He knew how to slow a song down so the audience would sing along.

They headed down Route 66 to Texas in Woody's car, on the way to Woody's family in Oklahoma. Together they composed songs like "66 Highway Blues," the first song Seeger ever completed. Woody gave Pete some tips on how to attract an audience.

They would arrive in a town and park outside the local bar. Then Woody would tell Pete to take his banjo out of the case, go inside, and order a drink. "Sooner or later somebody's gonna say, 'Hey kid, can you play that thing?' . . . Say, 'Well, not much.' . . . Pretty soon they'll say, 'Come on, kid, I'll give you a quarter if you'll play me a tune.'"

Soon Pete got the hang of performing on the road. When someone asked for music, Seeger would turn to face his listeners and play them a song. Together they made enough money to eat. One day Pete got a free haircut in exchange for a song.

After they reached Woody's family in Oklahoma, Pete headed back to Washington, D.C., to visit his father. But traveling didn't seem as exciting without Woody. Seeger said of his fellow musician that he often couldn't stand Woody when they were together but missed him when he was away. For his part, Woody noted in a set of New Year's resolutions that he needed to "28. Love Mama. 29. Love Papa. 30. Love Pete." The two men admired each other, and both struggled with their friendship. From Woody Pete gained a philosophy of performing: to sing not for fame or fortune but because you had something important to say.

Pete returned to New York City, the perfect place for a musician to work and meet other musicians. In the 1940s New York had a population of 7½ million; it boasted 600 theaters, three baseball teams, and dozens of daily papers, and it was the home of network radio—ideal for performers who wanted their songs heard all over America.

In New York Pete connected with Lee Hays, a tall, heavyset bass singer who was compiling labor songs. With Hays's songs and Seeger's banjo, they began to perform together. They sang their first gig in the Jade Mountain restaurant in New York. After that, Lee's roommate, Millard Lampell, a writer who could compose songs on the spot, joined them, as did baritone Pete Hawes. The group dubbed themselves the Almanac Singers and began performing, paying special attention to singing for union groups. Later, others became members of this flexible group of singers.

Until the labor movement began to gain strength in the 1930s, most Americans worked long hours for low wages every day of the week and had no power on the job. The labor movement took up the cause of improving working and living conditions for them. Workers in a specific trade, such as metalworkers or longshoremen, started forming unions to give themselves more power to negotiate with their bosses. Union members could fight collectively for better pay, better conditions, and shorter hours for workers. Improvements came slowly, but they came, including a shorter work week. As a present-day bumper sticker states, "The Labor Movement: The Folks Who Brought You the Weekend."

The Almanac Singers in performance in 1942. Left to right: Woody Guthrie, Millard Lampell, Bess Lomax Hawes, Pete Seeger, Arthur Stern, Sis Cunningham.

But improvements didn't come easily. When workers were desperate for better conditions and/or higher pay, a union might vote to strike, meaning that union members wouldn't show up to work. Company owners hated giving unions any power and fought against them. Still, strikers

in industry after industry began to refuse to work until they were given better conditions and higher pay. Before 1935, when the National Labor Relations Act was passed, employers were not required to negotiate with unions but could fire employees at will and bring in cheaper labor. Even after that, establishing unions in most industries often meant violent encounters between the owners and those they employed. The plight of American workers and the laborers' struggle engaged the young Pete Seeger.

In May 1941 the Almanac Singers tried out their repertoire before members of the Transport Workers Union, who were on strike against their employers. In honor of their audience, the group performed one of their signature songs, "Talking Union," and people roared in appreciation.

Pete had never received this kind of response for performing. Less than six months after the Almanac Singers was formed, Pete Seeger had found not only a group but a cause. He didn't want money; he didn't want fame; he didn't want trips to Hollywood. He wanted to play at union rallies. Some said his zeal for unions approached religious fervor. It was fortunate that Pete had no great expectations for recognition and money, as both were scarce. As the Almanacs traveled, they stayed in people's homes or cheap hotels "with enormous cockroaches in every room." They always worked as a group, copyrighting their songs collectively and taking turns singing the lead. They refused to list their individual names on album covers.

In July 1941 the Almanac Singers drove a run-down 1929 Buick, and Woody Guthrie joined them on the trip. They became cheerleaders for the American labor movement. At that moment about 2½ million union

In 1944 Pete entertained at the opening of the United Federal Labor Canteen in Washington, D.C. The event was sponsored by a union group, the Congress of Industrial Organizations (CIO). First lady Eleanor Roosevelt is seated in the center.

workers across the country were on strike. The Almanac Singers played concerts for them in Philadelphia, Pittsburgh, Cleveland, Chicago, and Milwaukee. They wrapped up their cross-country tour with a concert for dockworkers in San Francisco. Seeger, Lampell, and Guthrie stayed on the West Coast for a while, playing at picket lines, parties, and union meetings.

At Puget Sound, Washington, people hosted casual food and song parties that they called hootenannies. One person would bring a main dish such as beef stew; others brought side dishes and desserts. After the food, everyone danced and sang. Now Woody and Pete had a name for the kind of concert they liked to play.

Once all the Almanacs had returned to New York, they located a three-story house in Greenwich Village with a low rent, and they all moved in. Pete described their living conditions: "People came and went all the time. The cuisine was erratic but interesting . . . The output of songs was phenomenal."

Several other musicians moved in as well. The expanded group, long on talent but short on money, began holding Sunday-afternoon jam sessions that they called hootenannies. Lee Hays would bake bread, others brought food, and everyone attending threw in thirty-five cents to help pay the rent.

African American performers Brownie McGhee and Sonny Terry, a blind harmonica player from Georgia, sometimes joined the Almanacs in jam sessions and formal concerts. In the racially divided world of the 1940s, the Almanac members prided themselves on their diversity, long before the idea took root as a cause.

At a singing gig in New York, Pete met Toshi Ohta, whose name means "beginning of a new era" in Japanese. Toshi and Pete became friends and went out for hamburgers from time to time. Toshi stood a foot shorter than Pete and had shiny black hair and dark eyes. Opposites are said to attract, and Pete and Toshi were definitely physical opposites. But Pete, who hadn't dated many women, found himself extremely attracted to Toshi. Toshi's mother, who came from an old distinguished Virginia family, had married a Japanese exile and then gone to Europe to have her child. Because of the Oriental Exclusion Act, which prohibited children of 50 percent or more Oriental blood from entering the country, Toshi's mother had to smuggle her baby into America.

On December 7, 1941, the Japanese bombed the American naval base at Pearl Harbor in Hawaii, causing the United States to declare war on Japan and enter World War II. For someone who hated war like Pete Seeger, the decisions he now had to make were particularly difficult.

As they dated, Pete found himself falling in love with Toshi. But like other Americans of Japanese heritage, Toshi was now a target of hatred. Ostensibly to prevent sabotage, the United States government began rounding up Japanese American citizens and confining them to detention camps in the western states. Toshi's family escaped this indignity because they lived in the east.

Pete, who hated all wars, initially had been opposed to serving in the military. His antiwar songs included "Franklin D.," which declared, "You ain't gonna send me 'cross the sea," a jab at the current president, Franklin D. Roosevelt. But as the war progressed and after Adolf Hitler's German army invaded the Soviet Union, Pete's feelings began to change. Many of the singers he knew were engaged in the war effort; Woody

Guthrie joined the Merchant Marine; Pete decided he hated Hitler more than he loved the idea of staying out of the war. In June 1942, six months after Pearl Harbor, he received his draft notice for the army. His greatest regret was that he would be far away from Toshi.

In 1943, while still stationed in America, Pete took a temporary leave and married Toshi. Always efficient and quick to take charge, Toshi acquired the wedding ring (her grandmother's) and paid for the marriage license.

In one of his letters, Pete told Toshi that although he didn't drink or smoke, he did have an obsession—music—and he hoped she'd be patient with him. Toshi would prove more than patient. In that letter, Pete included a receipt, a record of an expenditure that he needed for filing taxes. She kept it and the thousands that followed so she could oversee their finances. She managed the details of Pete's career and served, sometimes formally and sometimes informally, as his manager. Toshi's practicality and focus would support and complement Pete for a lifetime. One friend in music said, decades later, "You want to know the difference between Seeger and some of the guys back then? . . . Maybe the biggest is having Toshi Ohta behind him—for seventy years!"

Eventually, Pete was transferred to the Special Services Division, a unit for performers, with its base at Fort Meade in Maryland, only a few hours from New York by train. Then, finally, in summer 1944, Pete

Taken between 1946 and 1948, this portrait photo shows Pete's enthusiasm and charm. But around this time, he was not having much success in his life as a musician. The photo is now in the National Portrait Gallery of the Smithsonian Museum.

was sent to the Pacific islands to provide hospital entertainment for wounded soldiers. During World War II Pete Seeger wasn't part of the combat troops, but he supported them with his unique skill—lifting the spirits of the soldiers by getting them to join in singing.

After the war ended in 1945, Pete returned to New York, and his friends noticed a change: more mature physically, he had also become a stronger singer. Always energetic, Pete took on a variety of projects. He established People's Songs, a union for singers. He taught classes, spoke at conferences, and composed music. Behind the scenes, Toshi kept everything running smoothly. She put food on the table for all those who came and went in their home.

Pete's efforts to build a musical career had left him full of passion but short on money. The Seegers had trouble paying the bills and were always poor. Pete often found he didn't even have a spare nickel and had to rely on Toshi's parents for financial support. He had learned about performing from Woody; he had found causes he believed in, like labor unions. But he couldn't find a way to be a musician and make enough money for Toshi, their young son, Danny, and their daughter, Mika. It looked as if he would have to add "became a singer" to his list of failures.

～ 5 ～
SUCCESS AT LAST

Last Saturday night I got married
Me and my love settled down
Now me and my love are parted
I'm gonna take another stroll downtown
Irene goodnight, Irene goodnight
Goodnight Irene, goodnight Irene
I'll see you in my dreams.
("Goodnight, Irene," traditional lyrics)

To ease some of his financial problems, Pete Seeger decided in 1949 that he and his family should leave New York City. He himself had been raised in a rural area, and he felt that Danny and Mika deserved to grow up close to nature. He also needed to take his family someplace where they could live on less money.

Pete and Toshi began to look for a home and found it near Beacon, New York. "By a great stroke of luck, Toshi and I were fortunate to find a few acres for sale on a wooded mountainside overlooking the Hudson, 60 miles north of the Big City." On this site Pete chopped down trees, opening a view of the Hudson River, and cleared land for a garden. After researching at the New York Public Library how to build log cabins, he began to dig trenches for a foundation. The first fall he wrote to a friend, artist Rockwell Kent, that the cold weather made sleeping outside difficult. So Pete's friend lent him a tent.

Other friends helped in the project. Scores of well-intentioned people came from the city; unfamiliar with country life, they were terrified by the copperhead snakes, bears, hordes of mosquitoes, and gargantuan spiders in the area. Pete set up speakers on the hillside so people could listen to music while they worked. His sixteen-year-old half sister Peggy arrived to be part of the work crew. She always remembered how at three o'clock one morning, Pete played recorded Amazon jungle noises and African desert sounds (howler monkeys, lions, and birds) at top volume. These sounds roused the fearful campers from their tents. He greeted them with his banjo and a song: "Wake up, wake up you lazy workers. What makes you sleep so sound?"

Friends from around the world came to visit and help. Czech filmmaker Gene Deitch did some roof work and helped boil maple syrup. Pete Seeger "must be the most generous musician on the planet," Deitch wrote. "He would never arrive at our house without his banjo and/or 12-string guitar. He always expected to play and be recorded. The only condition was that we sing with him, and he was pleased even if we— especially I—sang off-key!"

After years of being unable to support himself as a singer, Pete's luck began to change. Before he started constructing the house, Pete and Lee Hays, one of the Almanac Singers, had pulled together a quartet they called the Weavers. The other two members—Ronnie Gilbert, a young alto from Brooklyn with dramatic arched eyebrows, and Fred Hellerman, right out of Brooklyn College—were almost a decade younger than Hays and Seeger. Ronnie took the stage proudly and sang out confidently; at a time when most vocal groups were composed of men, she provided inspiration for young women everywhere. The four created a unique sound with their combination of voices—alto, split-tenor (a range between alto and tenor), baritone, and bass.

The Weavers: back, from left: Pete, Lee Hays, and Fred Hellerman; foreground, Ronnie Gilbert, 1953—at the time one of the most popular performing groups in the United States.

Initially, the Weavers didn't make much money. "We were dead broke and about to go our separate ways," Seeger remembered.

Then they were hired to play a short stint at a Greenwich Village club, the Village Vanguard, where they received two hundred dollars a week plus free hamburgers. Always hungry, Seeger ate so many hamburgers that the owners of the club decided to change the terms of his employment.

To try to help the group, Alan Lomax brought the famous American poet Carl Sandburg to hear them one night. Sandburg praised their efforts: "The Weavers are out of the grass roots of America. I salute them . . . When I hear America singing, the Weavers are there." When that quote hit the newspapers, everything changed. Crowds packed the club. The Weavers rarely performed a song the same way twice, but somehow every note they sang seemed just right.

Pete served as the spokesperson of the group and developed a unique style of introducing each song. He would strum on his banjo, soft and loud chords, while he said some words about the song. Then the music would begin. Pete would sing out with his strong, reedy voice; he was so animated in performance that he "looked like he was calling a moose." Millard Lampell, who had performed with the Almanac Singers, said of Seeger, "He wasn't the greatest banjo player, he didn't have the greatest voice, but there was something catchy about him." Pete Seeger had great rapport with his audiences; they trusted him and they loved him. While most singers try to make the music their own, Pete involved members of the audience so they would feel that the music belonged to them. In the words of singer Dave Van Ronk, "He genuinely respects the people who are listening to him. . . . He is not 'preserving' folklore but living it." Singer Arlo Guthrie, Woody's son, believed that the Weavers' strength came from "songs and stories—communication, not hype."

The Weavers focused on folk songs from around the world. They simplified them and produced something fresh and original. They looked for songs with powerful content. On one particularly memorable night, Pete stepped up to the microphone and announced a song from South Africa about the lost Lion King of the Zulus. "The legend holds that he didn't die, he simply went to sleep." Seeger led the audience in the refrain, "Way-up boy, Wimoweh, Wimoweh," and performed a marvelous Zulu yodel. Many years later, this song became part of the Disney movie and Broadway show *The Lion King*.

Gordon Jenkins of Decca Records attended a performance one night. He liked the way the Weavers simplified and streamlined musical arrangements and told stories with their music. At the end of the show, he invited the group to the Decca studio to take a look around. The Weavers released their first record with Decca, with "Tzena, Tzena" on one side and Lead Belly's song "Goodnight, Irene" on the other. Both songs headed to the top of the charts. The record sold four million copies within a year, more records than any pop song since World War II.

Pete remembered, "The summer of 1950, no American could escape that song ["Goodnight, Irene"] unless you plugged up your ears and went out in the wilderness someplace."

The Weavers transformed "Goodnight, Irene" into a best-selling popular song.

Great bookings started to flood in—big nightclubs like Ciro's in Hollywood, the Thunderbird Hotel in Las Vegas, the Palmer House in Chicago, and the Strand Theatre on Broadway. Pete went from working for hamburgers to making four thousand dollars a week. With their knack for taking the traditional and transforming it into something catchy and popular, the Weavers turned out one hit after another: "Wimoweh," "On Top of Old Smoky," "So Long, It's Been Good to Know Yuh." Some parts of this success bothered Pete, who now had to wear a tuxedo, which he disliked, when performing. One night he wore one green and one red sock in protest.

Toshi managed the Weavers, booking their appearances and buying their concert attire. In 1950 she accompanied the group on tour, leaving their young children, Danny and Mika, with her parents. When she returned, Danny didn't recognize her. After that, Toshi stayed home. She raised the children and fed the guests. She also protected the family from the limelight that surrounded Pete and kept family affairs private.

Pete came and went; sometimes he felt like a boarder when he came home. But the success of the Weavers meant that Pete was constantly in demand and—for the first time—making a great deal of money.

In 1950, at the height of the Weavers' success, it looked like the sky was the limit. Had their run continued, the group's record sales might have matched those of the most popular entertainers of the 1950s

Toshi Seeger at a Carnegie Hall concert in 1958. For a period of time Toshi served as the manager of the Weavers.

and 1960s, Elvis Presley and the Beatles. But trouble lay ahead for the Weavers. For as they sang about kisses sweeter than wine, a division of the United States government, the Federal Bureau of Investigation, had been keeping an eye on their activities.

~ 6 ~

UNDER SUSPICION

And for the cruel one who would tear out
This heart with which I live
I cultivate neither thistles nor nettles.
I cultivate a white rose.
(Translation of words of "Guantanamera"
by Jose Martí, adapted by Pete Seeger)

For years the FBI had been monitoring Pete Seeger and the other members of the Almanac Singers, calling the group "extremely untidy, ragged, and dirty in appearance." The director of the FBI, J. Edgar Hoover, must have believed in the power of song, because he and his bureau kept a vigilant watch over the activities of these singers.

While he was at Harvard, Pete had joined the Communist Youth League. During the 1940s he had been a member of the Communist Party of America—at a time when the Soviet Union was one of America's allies. Around 1949, realizing that communism in theory was quite different from what the government practiced in the Soviet Union, Pete ended his association with the CP-USA, as did many others. "I should have left much earlier," Pete said later. "I didn't examine closely enough what was going on." However, he remained throughout his life what he

During his long tenure as director of the FBI, J. Edgar Hoover wielded incredible power, using the information he gathered about everyone from presidents to ordinary citizens.

would call a "communist," with a small *c*, committed to the idea of people in a society sharing resources and wealth. For these political beliefs, Pete Seeger would be mercilessly persecuted.

In the late 1940s and early 1950s, fear of Communism had been building in America. After World War II the Soviet Union had expanded its territory to include many once-independent nations. Then in June 1950 the Korean War erupted, pitting America, which favored South Korea, against the Soviet Communists, who backed North Korea. *Red Channels: The Report of Communist Influence in Radio and Television* appeared that month, just as the Weavers' records climbed the charts. It named artists and entertainers allegedly attached to Communist-front associations: people such as actor-director Orson Welles, burlesque star Gypsy Rose Lee, playwrights Arthur Miller and Lillian Hellman, literary figures Dorothy Parker and Louis Untermeyer. Pete Seeger's name appeared among them.

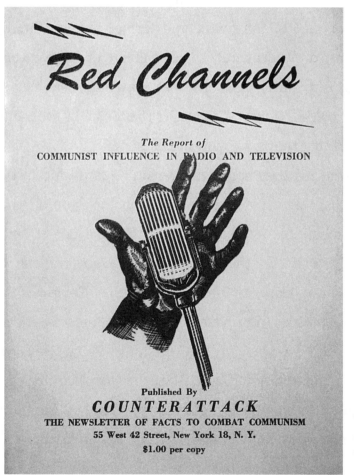

Red Channels: The Report of Communist Influence in Radio and Television was issued in 1950 by the right-wing publication *Counterattack*. It identified 151 actors, writers, journalists, and performers as Communists, including Pete Seeger.

By 1951 the Weavers increasingly faced ugly situations when they tried to perform. When they played in Ohio, people in the hotel lobby were reading newspaper headlines about "Weavers Named Reds." *The New York World-Telegram and Sun* ran an article on the group based on information in their FBI file. The Weavers' TV appearances were canceled by the networks, and the governor of Ohio got involved in making sure they didn't perform at the Ohio State Fair.

Harvey Matusow, an FBI informant and former member of the American Communist Party, ultimately sealed the fate of the Weavers. Like others, often called "stool pigeons," Matusow named names to keep himself out of trouble. He agreed to testify that he knew the members of this group and that they were Communists.

Matusow prepared his testimony with Senator Joseph McCarthy of Wisconsin, who had attracted public attention by claiming that there were large numbers of American Communist and Soviet spies in the United States, working for the overthrow of the government. In February 1952 Matusow appeared before a committee of Congress, the House Un-American Activities Committee. He testified under oath that three of the Weavers were members of the Communist Party. Lee Hays, he said, had been a member but had quit. Matusow also affirmed that Communists preyed on young people, ages four to six, rewriting nursery rhymes to indoctrinate them: "Jack Sprat could eat no fat, his wife could eat no lean/Because the Congress done them in and picked their pockets clean." Matusow later admitted in his book *False Witness* that there was no evidence of questionable political activity by Pete or other members of the group. They spent their time singing.

Matusow's false testimony discredited the Weavers and made them a focus of attack. Pete spoke up in defense of the group in a letter to the head of Decca Records, the label that released the Weavers' songs: "We have never in our lives knowingly participated in nor contributed to any action or cause disloyal to our country. . . . We're singers who make

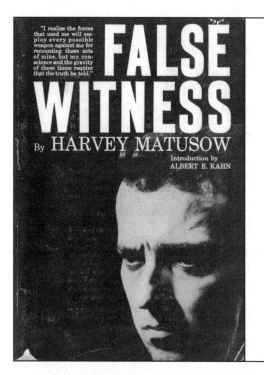

"I realize the forces that used me will employ every possible weapon against me for recounting these acts of mine, but my conscience and the gravity of these times require that the truth be told."

FALSE WITNESS

By HARVEY MATUSOW

Introduction by ALBERT E. KAHN

Affidavit of Harvey M. Matusow in the case of United States of America vs. Clinton E. Jencks, January 20, 1955.

IN THE DISTRICT COURT OF THE UNITED STATES
FOR THE WESTERN DISTRICT OF TEXAS
AT EL PASO

UNITED STATES OF AMERICA
vs.
CLINTON E. JENCKS

No. 54013
Criminal

HARVEY M. MATUSOW, being duly sworn, deposes and says:

1. I make this affidavit in support of the motion by the defendant for a new trial, and to do what I can to remedy the harm I have done to Clinton E. Jencks and to the administration of justice.

2. I appeared as a witness for the Government against the defendant in the course of the trial in this Court in January, 1954, on an indictment charging Mr. Jencks with having filed a false non-Communist affidavit with the National Labor Relations Board on April 28, 1950. My testimony appears in the typewritten transcript of the record from p. 579 to p. 703.

3. The matters I testified to were either false or not entirely true, and were known by me to be either false or not entirely true, at the time I so testified, in that:

In *False Witness*, Harvey Matusow admitted that he had provided false information about Pete Seeger and others.

recordings of the best American folk songs we know. . . . We collect and arrange songs, and we write new ones. This is all we do." But it made no difference.

Like others accused of Communist leanings at the time, the Weavers found it almost impossible to get work. If the group tried to rent a hall for a concert, the person who owned the hall got a call saying, "Did you know that you're renting your hall to the Communist?" Quickly the deposit would be returned. Finally the Weavers had to play at locations like Daffy's Bar and Grill outside of Cleveland. The American Legion tried to get the owner of Daffy's to cancel. Although the Weavers had sold over four million records, they could not find a hall where they could guarantee a performance. In 1953 Decca stopped releasing their records and removed every mention of the group from their catalogue.

Mysterious fires broke out on the Seegers' property; strangers were seen lurking close to their home; tension developed with neighbors who did not want to be near Communists. Toshi and the children, Danny, Mika, and baby Tinya, lived with constant anxiety. Pete put a brave face on what was happening. He reassured his mentor and friend Woody Guthrie, "Toshi and I aren't scared."

But plenty of people were scared, many of them children. Between 1919, when the Communist Party was founded in the United States, and 1956, hundreds of thousands of Americans had become party members or joined party-led organizations. Their children were often called red

A family portrait, from left: Mika, Toshi, Tinya, Danny, and Pete.

diaper babies, red being the color of the Communist flag. Although every child's experience was unique, all of them faced similar problems. Many were instructed never to answer the phone or open the door. Others were afraid their parents might be put in jail, or that they might be tortured themselves to give information.

Sometimes federal agents or watchers in unmarked cars parked outside homes. If no one was there, agents would enter a home to look for compromising material. Telephone conversations were recorded.

Agents tailed the children of those under investigation to playgrounds, parties, picnics, and ball games. The government was doing its best to intimidate the families, and often the friends, of those suspected of Communist sympathies.

In the 1950s the House Un-American Activities Committee, known as HUAC or "the Committee," brought in one American citizen after another and grilled each of them about their friends and associates. American citizens who had done no wrong "felt the same sickening terror that victims of a dictatorship know." After Matusow testified, Pete realized he would eventually be called before the Committee and possibly sent to jail. He and his family waited for the inevitable summons from HUAC. Pete's battles to clear himself of these false charges would last, in fact, for a decade.

~ 7 ~

FIGHTING BACK

Michael, row the boat ashore,
Hallelujah!
Then you'll hear the trumpet blow
Hallelujah!
(Traditional spiritual)

During those terrible years, Pete Seeger did what he did best—took action and kept moving. In the 1950s he waged the most important battle of his life: fighting for his right to sing.

The Weavers tried to continue as a group; they presented a few more concerts. But Pete, now in his thirties, decided to leave the group and perform on his own. He went underground. He barnstormed across the country, playing in small colleges and churches, collecting supporters and fans. He carried his banjo to forty states and performed at hundreds of concerts, even though he might get only twenty-five dollars each time. He also went back to singing for children in schools and summer camps, as he had at the beginning of his career. He sang about brotherhood and sisterhood and included songs from around the world.

To support himself and his family, Pete returned to what he knew best: playing his banjo and singing songs.

Pete shared with his young listeners the idealistic belief in a world that could be made better by collective action.

He even enjoyed his role as a rebel. Pete would call up a radio station,

The ever-energetic Pete Seeger took his banjo to schools and summer camps, where he played for children and college students.

get a spot on the air, and then be out of town before the American Legion could protest. He also wrote a column in *Sing Out!*, a publication about folk music, which he dedicated to the thousands of boys and girls who had started to carry folk songs throughout the land. As he said, the American folk hero John Chapman, known as Johnny Appleseed, traveled for fifty years, planting apple seeds and seedlings across the American frontier. In effect, Pete became the Johnny Appleseed of folk music. He traveled thousands of miles across the country, passing along his songs to the young.

Pete wrote hundreds of columns for *Sing Out!* over the years. He and Lee Hays were featured on the cover in 1976.

During this period Pete developed a song he called "Abiyoyo." It tells the story of a father and son who are outcasts from their community. Their skills—making things disappear and playing the ukulele—are considered useless. But then they are called upon to use these talents to defeat a giant. Although Pete faced attacks during the McCarthy years, he believed that someday he would be needed and valued. The story's hopeful theme would sustain him through dark times and foreshadowed part of his own life.

In August 1955 Pete Seeger and some of his friends were raising the walls for a barn on his property when a shiny black car came up the driveway.

"Are you Pete Seeger?" the man asked. "I've got something for you."

The man handed Pete the subpoena he had been expecting for three and a half years—a legal document requiring him to testify before the House Un-American Activities Committee. Performing "Abiyoyo" for children shortly after receiving this summons, Seeger said, "Some good stories have a moral; here, one good song [by the ukulele player] beat a giant. Next week, I'll be questioned by some men who want me to stop singing."

After choosing a lawyer and deciding on a strategy, Seeger went to face the Committee. A lot had changed since 1952. The Korean War had ended, lessening the tension over Communism in the United States. A year before, Senator McCarthy had been condemned on the floor of the

After Harvey Matusow testified that Pete was a Communist, Pete appeared with his lawyer, Paul Ross, before the House Un-American Activities Committee.

Senate for his devious tactics and abuse of power. By now HUAC's influence was decreasing. Most of the Committee activities simply included the harassment of American citizens. Throughout its seventeen-year history, "No blacklisted [under suspicion; to be boycotted] American was ever found to have been engaged in plotting the overthrow of the government. None was found to have been a spy."

Most of those who appeared before the Committee declined to answer questions, citing the Fifth Amendment of the Constitution, which says that Americans cannot be forced to incriminate themselves. Although this is a legitimate defense, many of these citizens were described by the press as "Fifth Amendment" Communists. But Pete was attracted to a different stand. He wanted to claim First Amendment rights. He felt that he had a right to his personal beliefs and that that he was being punished without reason. By bringing in the First Amendment, Pete would be declaring that this committee of Congress had no right to ask anyone questions about their personal beliefs. The Hollywood Ten, a group of screenwriters and movie directors, had tried this approach earlier, had spent time in jail, and had been on the blacklist for years.

Pete's defense essentially challenged the approach of the Committee, but it put him at great risk. In 1955, when Pete appeared before the Committee, he boldly stated: "I am not going to answer any questions as to my association, my philosophical or religious beliefs or my political beliefs, or how I voted in any election or any of these private affairs. I think these are very improper questions for any American to be asked." He then said: "I feel that in my whole life I have never done anything of any conspiratorial nature and I resent very much and very deeply the implication of being called before this Committee that in some way because my opinions may be different from yours . . . that I am any less of an American than anybody else. I love my country very deeply, sir."

When asked whether his song "Wasn't That a Time" was subversive, he offered to play what he considered a deeply patriotic song, but the Committee refused to listen. After he left the Committee, Pete sang "Wasn't That a Time" for assembled reporters and television cameramen, who filmed it for the nightly news. His manager, Harold Leventhal, joked that it was a terrible way to get a song on the air.

In July 1956 the House of Representatives of the United States of America voted 373 to 9 to cite Pete Seeger and seven others for contempt of Congress. While he waited to learn at his next trial whether or not he would be jailed, Pete kept busy. He wrote the beautiful ballad "Where Have All the Flowers Gone?" He continued writing columns for *Sing Out!*, bringing little-known folk songs such as "Michael, Row Your Boat Ashore" and "Guantanamera" to the attention of his readers.

In the long run Pete's battle with HUAC made him a hero. While singing across the country in small venues, he built a legion of fans. Many who had been devoted to him as children had grown up to become his staunchest supporters. Thousands came to the concerts of a man who—just like the folk heroes he sang about—challenged the establishment. Some of those young listeners became advocates of telling inconvenient truths themselves. At a concert in Palo Alto in 1954, singers Joan Baez and Dave Guard, later of the Kingston Trio, heard Pete Seeger and

Pete Seeger, with his banjo slung over his back, arrives in federal court, 1961.

decided to follow in his footsteps. Singers John Mellencamp and Bruce Springsteen fell under his spell. Pete inspired and performed with Arlo Guthrie, Woody's son, who had also become a musician. Not only was Pete's music exciting, Pete personally inspired people. As an artist, he never sold out. He never compromised.

In March 1961, in New York City, Pete Seeger went on trial for contempt of Congress. He was sentenced to ten years in jail, handcuffed by the bailiff, and locked in a cell. Released on bail a few hours later, Pete and his lawyers immediately began the process of appealing his conviction. Finally, ten years after the persecution of Pete Seeger began, in May 1962 the U.S. Court of Appeals ruled that his indictment was faulty and dismissed the case.

Pete had been vindicated. Having faced legal hassles for a decade, he had always believed that in the end things would work out for the best. Later he would say of those years, "When you're following what you think is the right course, it may not be fun, but you feel a certain satisfaction in doing it."

~ 8 ~

JOINING FORCES

We will overcome,
We will overcome,
We will overcome someday.
Oh, deep in my heart,
I do believe
We will overcome someday.
("We Will Overcome," traditional lyrics)

With legal battles behind him, Pete Seeger could apply his full energy to causes that he cared about. Now he didn't have to ask a federal judge for permission when he wanted to travel farther than New Jersey. In the 1960s the push for full voting rights for blacks took center stage; then protest against America's involvement in the Vietnam War intensified. Pete Seeger used his voice to sing for civil rights and peace.

In October 1962 he headed south to Albany, Georgia. A pray-in at the Albany city hall had brought the charismatic African American preacher Martin Luther King Jr. to town, and King had been arrested with seventy-five other members of the clergy. One civil rights organizer had been shot; a church had been burned to the ground. The community

From left to right: Dr. Martin Luther King, Pete Seeger, Charis Horton, Rosa Parks, and the Rev. Ralph Abernathy at Highlander Folk School, Knoxville, Tennessee, where Pete first heard the song "We Will Overcome." He altered it slightly, and it became the protest anthem of the civil rights movement.

invited Seeger to perform protest songs at a church so they could learn from a veteran.

A group of local citizens drove sedans around the church, ready to create trouble. Whites carrying lead pipes taunted the churchgoers as they entered. Inside, Seeger had a hard time connecting with the audience until he led them in a protest anthem originally named "We Will Overcome." The song had been sung by striking black tobacco workers in North Carolina. Pete had heard it first in 1947. He had changed "we will" to "we shall" because he liked the way "shall" sang, opening the mouth a bit wider.

He had also added new verses, including "We'll walk hand in hand" and "We shall live in peace."

In Albany Seeger engaged his listeners with "We Shall Overcome." They held hands and swayed to the music. With this song, he was trying to reflect the hopes and dreams of those in the church. Changed and embellished by Pete, the anthem became a favorite of Martin Luther King and eventually the identifying song of the civil rights movement.

When Seeger's legal troubles ended, his passport, confiscated while he was on trial, was returned to him. His manager, Harold Leventhal, and Toshi arranged a world tour. Setting out in August 1963, Pete, Toshi, and their children visited twenty-two countries in ten months. Pete performed for enraptured audiences in Western Samoa, Japan, Kenya, Nigeria, Ghana, Israel, Czechoslovakia, and Ireland. In his forties, Pete still looked like a boy onstage. His infectious ability to get an audience singing with him, to bring people together, worked its magic throughout the world.

The first stop on the tour was Melbourne, Australia, where Pete appeared to wildly enthusiastic crowds. The first thing Pete did when he walked onstage at the Melbourne Town Hall was to dedicate the concert to the children in the audience. "Kids know more than grownups anyway," he quipped. "It was a child who said, 'Someday they will hold a war and nobody will come.'" At first the audience sang hesitantly, lips barely moving; by the end of the performance they harmonized, joined in, and even yodeled.

Back in the United States, Pete stepped up his protest activities. In June 1964 the Mississippi Summer Project—sponsored by several organizations including Martin Luther King's Southern Christian Leadership

Pete with fellow activists at a civil rights rally in Greenwood, Mississippi, 1963.

Conference—was helping blacks register to vote in the South. From the beginning, those involved in the project, who came from all over the country, were threatened with violence. Pete Seeger was performing in Meridian, Mississippi, when word came that the bodies of three project workers had been found buried in a dam. He led a weeping audience in "We Shall Overcome." On March 24, 1965, he joined King in a protest march to Selma, Alabama—again to bring media attention to the denial of voting rights to blacks. He said later, "What am I accomplishing? some will ask . . . I'd rather throw my weight, however small, on the side of what I think is right than selfishly look after my own fortunes."

During the 1960s Pete continued to perform for young children and college audiences. "There's nothing like a crisis to bring out the urge to write poetry," he wrote later. "Every week I was singing at different colleges and was able to test out a new song on a live-wire audience. I knew I was doing O.K. when some person would loudly boo a line and then was promptly drowned out by thousands of cheers."

One person typical of the time described her childhood memory of Seeger. "In the early 1960s when I was about ten, I saw Pete Seeger in concert. He was performing on the porch of a big house, and I was seated on the lawn, almost at his feet. I sang lustily along with the rest of the audience. I so wanted him to ask that little girl in the front row with the glasses to come up and sing with him! I have never forgotten seeing him; I was in awe."

Pete continued to be a powerful influence on younger singers as well. Many of his earlier songs were recorded in the 1960s by those making a name for themselves. He had written and first performed the powerful antiwar ballad "Where Have All the Flowers Gone?" in 1955. Then Peter, Paul, and Mary and the Kingston Trio made it a hallmark antiwar song. Joan Baez, already an admirer, would use it as her signature song for the next forty-five years. Popular singer Judy Collins made Seeger's song "Turn, Turn, Turn" a hit.

Frustrated with America's growing involvement in Vietnam, Seeger turned to writing new songs of protest. He and Toshi had three children of mixed racial descent. He was haunted by pictures of the burned children in Vietnam. The killing of those children felt personal to him, emotionally close to home. He wrote a song about a platoon of soldiers in Louisiana in 1942 performing an army exercise. Although the men are waist deep in a river called the Big Muddy, "the big fool [their captain] says to push on" into deeper water. Although he was ostensibly writing about World War II, Seeger was thinking about the current conflict. The song was taken up by opponents of the Vietnam War. Then he began performing another antiwar song, addressed to all Americans, about the troops who were fighting in Vietnam: "Bring 'Em Home." As the antiwar movement gained strength across the country, young people protested on college campuses; sit-ins, demonstrations, tear gas, riots, and gunfire rocked once-sleepy academic towns.

Seeger's antiwar stance also resonated strongly with many of those being asked to fight in the war.

Although Seeger had been cleared of all legal charges, television producers remained wary. He had been asked to perform on ABC-TV but would be required to sign a loyalty oath. He refused, believing such oaths unconstitutional, and the invitation was withdrawn. Finally, in 1967, he was invited to perform on CBS's popular variety show *The Smothers Brothers Comedy Hour.* On the show, which was taped, he sang a group of soldiers' songs, including "John Brown's Body." He ended the performance with "Waist Deep in the Big Muddy."

Host Tommy Smothers introduced Seeger to millions of American households. During the show, Smothers had asked Pete if he was going to sing "Waist Deep in the Big Muddy," and Pete did. But the videotape of the show was censored by CBS executives, who cut the song from the tape. Seeger said after viewing that show: "One moment I had a guitar in my hand; a second later I had a banjo in my hand—it was an obvious cut." Pete Seeger was no longer blacklisted, but he was still denied his right to be heard.

In November 1969 Pete joined the March on Washington, D.C., protesting the Vietnam War. A half million people crowded the Capitol area. Seeger tried to lead them in "Bring 'Em Home," but the song was too complex for responsive singing. Then he tried something else. "I decided it was worth a gamble to try the short refrain by Yoko Ono and

Pete never lost his boyish charm and unpretentious manner, as this photograph taken in 1968 shows.

John Lennon, which I'd heard only three days before." He led the crowd in singing "All we are saying is give peace a chance," only ten seconds long. "We sang it over and over. After 30 seconds a few thousand were singing it with us. After a minute tens of thousands. . . . Looking out at that sea of faces, it was like a huge ballet, flags, banners, signs, would move to the right for three beats (one measure) and then left for the next measure . . . A litany! . . . Finally we let it end softly as in a gospel church when a hymn has been sung till no one can add more."

This occasion was one of the most extraordinary experiences of Pete Seeger's life. "The sight was tremendous, to see hundreds of thousands of people swaying forward from right to left." In that moment he realized that he wasn't sure what was being accomplished by the event, but he did know "that either we are all going to make it together or none of us will make it."

In the end, the civil rights protests helped secure voting rights for blacks throughout the United States. Antiwar protests shortened the duration of America's involvement in the Vietnam War. Pete Seeger lent his voice, his talent, his skill as a songwriter, and his passion to these movements and gave Americans some of their greatest protest songs.

Had Pete Seeger's activism ended in the early 1960s, he would have accomplished enough for a lifetime. But he was not done yet.

～ 9 ～

SINGING TOGETHER TO
SAVE OUR PLANET

A ship there was, and she sailed the sea,
She's loaded deep, as deep can be.
But not as deep as the love I'm in
And I know not how, I sink or swim.
("The Water Is Wide," traditional lyrics)

Pete Seeger had always functioned best fighting real enemies —those who tried to keep unions from organizing, the House Un-American Activities Committee, officials denying voting rights to black Americans. Just causes also brought out his energy and creativity. In the 1960s a local political issue launched his next initiative. He discovered an important cause in his own backyard—or rather, the river that ran past his backyard. This time he would "Think globally, act locally." He was going to clean up the Hudson River.

At the same time, Pete began to feel he needed to make some friends in his community. He had been warmly welcomed all over the United States and around the world, but he had had friction with people closer to home. After the Peekskill concert (presented at the beginning of this book), those who lived nearby had thrown rocks at Pete and his family. In another painful incident, seven hundred people in Pete's town of Beacon, New York, signed a petition requesting that he not appear at the local high school. But now he was ready to leave the unpleasantness behind.

With the river close at hand, Pete fell in love with sailing. It wasn't all that scenic, however. "Sailing on the Hudson, I saw lumps of toilet waste floating past me." The Hudson River was filthy, coated with an oil slick, a dumping ground for old tires, refuse, and industrial waste. Every time Pete drove along the shore of the Hudson, he could smell chemicals. He sailed on the river anyway, imagining what it could be if it were cleaned up.

A neighbor, Vic Schwartz, lent him a book titled *Sloops of the Hudson*, written in 1908. As a child, Pete had taken pleasure in building wooden boats with his father's tools. He became enchanted with the idea of building a life-size replica of a Hudson River sloop, in the style favored by the early Dutch settlers.

Then he created a grand plan that linked building a sloop, cleaning up the river, and involving everyone along the Hudson.

First, Seeger and Schwartz set about getting money to build a Hudson River sloop. They began with a fundraiser concert for 160 people, where they passed the hat and collected $160. A lawyer volunteered his services and got them nonprofit status as "Clearwater." A step at a time, a person at a time, a dollar at a time, Pete Seeger gathered enough support to keep the project going. Performing at benefit concerts on people's lawns up and down the Hudson, he raised the $140,000 they would need to start construction. Finally, Pete oversaw the building of a wooden sloop at a shipyard in Maine. It was made of oak, weighed a hundred tons, was 25 feet wide and 76 feet long, and had a mast that stood 106 feet in the air. Called the *Clearwater*, the boat was the first of its kind to be created in eighty years.

On June 17, 1969, the *Clearwater* sailed into the Atlantic, piloted by a group of musicians. They played their first concert in Portland, Maine, and worked their way down the coast. When they sailed into New York's East River, crowds gathered to see the boat. Tugboats pulled alongside the boat, sounding their horns. Helicopters with TV news crews flew overhead. "The price of liberty is eternal publicity," said Pete. "And we're getting it." They were also raising funds for the next part of the campaign; the maiden voyage made $27,000.

A boat, a vision, a mission. Pete proudly acknowledged this early success. "What can a song do? What can a sailboat do? . . . In the summer of 1969, they helped clean up a river."

Then Pete Seeger did what he always did for his causes: he wrote songs, including "Sailing on the Golden River" and "Garbage," which he played on *The Today Show*. Slowly the Hudson became cleaner, one piece of garbage removed at a time. The group took General Electric to court over the illegal dumping of PCBs (polychlorinated biphenyl, a

The *Clearwater* in full sail.

cancer-inducing chemical) in the Hudson River and won the case. Pete claimed, "A few committed individuals can change the world. It is the only thing that ever has." And he had proved it once again.

The Beacon Sloop Club was Seeger's next campaign. The building he chose as its headquarters was an abandoned diner, damp and cold and dark. Slowly those Pete attracted to the club began transforming it just as they were altering the river, a bit at a time. The club became the means to raise money for the boat. When the strawberries got ready to be picked in June, they had a strawberry festival; when corn ripened in

August, they had a corn festival; in October, a pumpkin festival. Pete would work right alongside the people picking crops in the field, telling them stories.

People only mourn the loss of what they have learned to love, as early environmentalists like Aldo Leopold claimed in *Sand County Almanac*. To help children grow to know and care about the river, Pete captained the *Clearwater* one day a week, and crews of children, often as many as fifty at a time, came aboard to learn about the environment. They would arrive in a bus from school, do whatever work the captain requested, such as hauling on the lines to pull up the sails, and fish in the river. They experienced being on the river, observing water birds, and enjoying the beauty of the land.

When Pete Seeger turned ninety, in May 2009, he made his birthday celebration a fundraising event for Clearwater. Some 18,000 fans headed to Madison Square Garden to wish Pete many more winters, as the spokesperson for the Iroquois Nation phrased it. Joan Baez, John Mellencamp, Arlo Guthrie, and Bruce Springsteen were among those who gathered to pay homage to a man who had fought for his beliefs and yet never descended into bitterness. All the funds raised went to helping keep the Hudson River clean and children sailing on this golden river.

With the Clearwater project, Pete Seeger became an advocate for the green revolution, the movement to save our planet and environment. One of his favorite ideas involved the ordinary caulk gun, a staple

Thousands of friends and well-wishers attended Pete's ninetieth birthday concert at Madison Square Garden in New York City, May 6, 2009. Pete displays his famous banjo, inscribed with the words "THIS MACHINE SURROUNDS HATE AND FORCES IT TO SURRENDER."

in many houses, which he believed could be one of the most important tools in our world. Thirty percent of a home's heat efficiency is lost through cracks; caulking those cracks would reduce the use of fossil fuels for heating. Like so many of Seeger's ideas, his proposed solution was within the reach of everyone. As a child Pete Seeger had loved the ideas of Ernest Thompson Seton about living in harmony with the land. As an adult he became a crusader for the environmental movement—lending his voice, his songs, and his energy to preserving the natural world.

Seeger liked to tell a story about two frogs: "A farmer once left a tall can of milk with the top off outside his door. Two frogs hopped into it and then found that they couldn't hop out. After thrashing around a bit, one of them says, 'There's no hope.' With one last gurgle he sank to the bottom. The other frog refused to give up. In the morning the farmer came out and found one live frog sitting on a big cake of butter." Like the second frog, whose efforts had churned the milk into butter, Pete Seeger refused to give up.

～ 10 ～
PETE SEEGER'S LEGACY

A time to be born, a time to die
A time to plant, a time to reap
A time to kill, a time to heal.
A time to laugh, a time to weep.
(Words from the Book of Ecclesiastes,
adapted for the song "Turn, Turn, Turn" by Pete Seeger)

On January 18, 2009, on the steps of the Lincoln Memorial in Washington, D.C., Pete Seeger, almost ninety years old, stood—tall, lean, and trim from his daily regime of wood chopping—at the inaugural concert for President Barack Obama. He encouraged a million people to sing along with him. Bruce Springsteen introduced Pete Seeger to an adoring audience with the words, "Here is the father of American folk music." Wearing no coat despite the freezing weather, sporting a striped shirt and an off-kilter colorful wool cap, and carrying a banjo adorned with the words THIS MACHINE SURROUNDS HATE AND FORCES IT TO SURRENDER, the vibrant and energetic performer fed the crowd the lyrics of one of Woody Guthrie's songs, "This Land Is Your Land." "Even the press corps sang along," said NPR reporter Allison Keyes. "Everyone's mouth was moving"—including President Obama's.

In that same city, several decades earlier, Seeger had been called before HUAC for his political beliefs. But he continued to sing his songs and let his voice be heard. From persecuted singer to adored American icon, Pete Seeger represented the best of America. He kept going; he persevered; he remained optimistic and committed.

Over time—just as the story of Abiyoyo predicted—people realized

In 1994 Pete Seeger was awarded the National Medal of Arts by President Clinton. Also honored were actress Julie Harris and singer Harry Belafonte.

that they needed Pete Seeger. They needed him to slay the giants. They needed his integrity and his ability to tell inconvenient truths. They needed him to do what he had been doing all along—singing about freedom and justice.

Just as he had hoped he would in childhood, Pete Seeger became many things in his life. He was an author, an activist, a tireless advocate of human dignity, equal rights, and peace; and above all he gave a voice to the feelings and hopes of people all over the world. At a conservative estimate, Pete Seeger performed live for five million people in forty different countries. A preacher who used his banjo to deliver his sermons, he got people excited about music for seven decades. In his last few years, scores of accolades came to him—a Grammy, the Presidential Medal of Honor, election to the Rock and Roll Hall of Fame. Year after year adoring fans all over the globe nominated him for a Nobel Peace Prize. And when Pete died on January 27, 2014, about six months after his wife, Toshi, personal and official tributes flooded in from all over the world, attesting to his influence and his remarkable character.

In his lifetime Pete was never swayed by awards or personal recognition. He worked for the causes he supported and never stopped believing that the right song, at the right time, could change history. In his nineties he continued to express his views, even when he couldn't stand or walk without canes. On October 21, 2011, Pete Seeger joined a crowd of a thousand people as Occupy Wall Street, a protest against big business, moved through New York City. Accompanied by his grandson Tao Rodriguez Seeger, and supported by two canes, Pete performed with Arlo Guthrie the protest anthem "We Shall Overcome." At one point a policeman grabbed Tao Seeger and asked, "Was this your idea?" Pete's grandson was afraid he was going to be arrested. Instead, the officer shook his hand and said, "This is beautiful."

Leading a musician's life on the road, Pete Seeger had to leave his family much of the time; one year he was home only 90 days out of the 365. But he was able to be present for his grandchildren: Tao, Kitama, Cassie Moraya, Penny, and Isabelle. A talented musician in his own right, Tao, Mika's son, began performing with his grandfather when Pete started losing his voice. Pete's grandson Kitama Cahill-Jackson, Tinya's son and a filmmaker, celebrated Pete in a powerful documentary, *Pete Seeger: The Power of Song*. Staying close to home and chopping wood every day, Pete passed on his wisdom to the next generations of Seegers.

Throughout his life Pete Seeger remained committed to the idea that people need to come together. "It's been my life's work, to get participation, whether it's a union song, a peace song, civil rights, or women's movement, or gay liberation. When you sing, you feel, I'm not alone."

Support for workers. Peace. The right to speak and sing in freedom. Civil rights for all people. The preservation of the planet. The causes to which Pete Seeger dedicated his life remain relevant and evergreen. He lived with purpose and meaning. As he often said, "Nobody really knows what the world's going to bring. . . . We always find solutions, we're an intelligent race . . . As long as I've got breath, I'll keep on doing what I can."

His life stands as a testament for social and political change, reminding everyone to fight for what they believe in and to let their voices be heard.

AFTERWORD

Pete Seeger was one of my heroes when I was a teenager. I played the guitar (badly), sang his songs, and admired his spirit. Before I began this project several years ago, I talked to him to make sure he felt comfortable about having this biography written. One of the happiest days in my life came when Pete, after several conversations, gave me his blessing to work on this book. A few months later he said, "Take your time. Write a good book. I will probably be dead by the time you finish." In this, as in so many other things, he was right.

Fortunately for me as a researcher, there is an abundance of primary source materials about Pete Seeger. He wrote many books about his life and gave thousands of interviews. I also had the opportunity to interview him. And, as I learned in the process of working on this book, almost everyone I talked to had at least one Pete Seeger story. When possible, I have used Pete Seeger's own words as he recorded them. The dialogue in these pages comes directly from Pete Seeger's various accounts of what he said and what was said to him. None of this dialogue was invented by me.

Biographers have a responsibility to examine the facts, remain as unbiased as possible, and tell the truth about their subjects. Certainly that is the spirit in which I undertook this project. But I would misrepresent myself if I claimed to have remained neutral. When I read the files that the FBI had gathered about Pete Seeger, and I studied the complete testimony of Pete Seeger's appearance before the House Un-American Activities Committee, I became angry and disturbed. How could someone who had given so much to society, someone as selfless as Pete Seeger, be harassed and mistreated by the American government? When I read accounts by those who had been children in this era, the so-called red diaper babies, I was outraged. How could children be treated this way by agents of their own government? In many ways those children were the innocent victims of those grim times.

Although Pete Seeger never grew bitter, I am still disturbed by what happened to him during the 1950s and 1960s—this devoted professional who just wanted to sing songs. I offer up his story in the hope that as a nation we never again turn on our own citizens and do them the same kind of injustice.

Anita Silvey

Westwood, Massachusetts

SOURCE NOTES

All materials referred to in the Notes can be found in the Bibliography on page 96.

Abbreviations used:

Abiyoyo: Seeger, *Abiyoyo*

Clearwater: *The Clearwater Concert*

Dunway: Dunway, *How Can I Keep from Singing?*

Flowers: Seeger, *Where Have All the Flowers Gone?*

Incompleat: Seeger, *Incompleat Folksinger*

Rosenthal: Rosenthal and Rosenthal, *Pete Seeger*

Van Ronk: Van Ronk, *The Mayor of MacDougal Street*

Wilkinson: Wilkinson, *The Protest Singer: An Intimate Portrait of Pete Seeger*

Willens: Willens, *Lonesome Traveler*

Introduction

1-2 "When the concert . . . was broken": *Incompleat*, 464–65

1. *The Beginnings*

3-8 Seeger family: Dunway, 17–28

4 "Other relatives . . . crackpots": Rosenthal, 5

5 *Alan Seeger*: Dunway, 25

6 They traveled slowly: *Flowers*, 282

The Seegers quickly learned: Dunway, 31

7 Traveling around the country: *Flowers*, 11; Dunway, 31

8 "We're having . . . mother?": Dunway, 32

But Pete's life changed: Dunway, 32

2. Mentors and School

10 "*Once . . . here!*" Abiyoyo, [6]

Native Americans as models: *Incompleat*, 246

11-12 "I saved . . . university": Pete Seeger, essay in *Everything I Need to Know I Learned from a Children's Book*

12 Pete Seeger's relationship with his father: Dunway, 35–36, 38

Pete's mother: Rosenthal, 8–9

12-13 Avon Old Farms: *Flowers*, 101; Dunway, 40–41

12-16 Pete as a child and music: *Flowers*, 11

13 "The banjo . . . going on?": Clearwater

14 "Give me . . . banjo": Twain, "Enthusiastic Eloquence"

15 "typing, writing . . . questions": *Incompleat*, 559

pet snake: Dunway, 43

traveling with his father: *Incompleat*, 13

Asheville, North Carolina.: *From the Blue Ridge Mountains: Give me the Banjo*. PBS Arts Festival

"These songs . . . honest": *Incompleat*, 13

love . . . injustice: Rosenthal, 12

16 "I never . . . sing it": *Incompleat*, 62

Harvard: Dunway, 52–55

Harvard dropouts: Tom Moroney, "Facebook's Zuckerberg Becomes Latest Harvard Dropout to Drop In"

3. Choosing Music

18 watercolor painting: Rosenthal, 12

farmer or a forest ranger: Alan Wilkinson, "The Protest Singer," *The New Yorker*

19 "I play . . . to that": Dunway, 61

Dalton School: Dunway, 56–61

"I started . . . painter": Rosenthal, 36

Alan Lomax: Dunway, 64–65; Kappers, *Lomax the Songhunter*

21 Huddie Ledbetter: Rosenthal, 55; *Pete Seeger: Live in Australia 1963*, DVD; "Two Links of a Chain: The Story of Lead Belly as Told by Pete Seeger"

22 work at Library of Congress: *Incompleat*, 230

"instrumental and . . . U.S.A.," "cowboys . . . gangs": *Flowers*, 12

"ambled . . . made up": Dunway, 67

24 Woody and Pete: Rosenthal, 14

trip: Dunway, 69

4. Becoming a Performer

25-26 Woody Guthrie and Pete Seeger: Dunway, 72–73; *Flowers*, 17

"Sooner . . . tune": Dunway, 75

free haircut: Dunway, 71

Pete . . . Woody: Dunway, 98

"28. Love . . . Pete": "Woody Guthrie's New Year's Resolutions from 1942," *American Songwriter*

Pete Seeger and Woody: Seeger, *Pete Remembers Woody*

27 the Almanac Singers: Dunway, 81–82, 86

"The Labor . . . weekend": Northlands Poster

30 Pete's enthusiasm for unions: Dunway, 85–86

"with enormous . . . room": Rosenthal, 20

31 The Almanac Singers's tour: Dunway, 98

32 "People . . . phenomenal": *Incompleat*, 17

Toshi Ohta: Dunway, xx, 58–59, 108

33 "Franklin D.": Dunway, 92

34 Pete's decision to fight: Rosenthal, 131

Toshi and Pete's relationship: Dunway, 122–23; Rosenthal, xvi

"You want . . . years!": Dunway, 122–23

36 After the war: Dunway, 133, 137, 154

5. *Success at Last*

37 "By . . . Big City": *Flowers*, 45

38 Rockwell Kent: Dunway, 158–59

Peggy Seeger testimony: Clearwater

"must be . . . off-key!": Deitch, "The 65 Greats behind the Scenes"

39 The Weavers: Dunway, 160; Willens, 110

40 "We were . . . ways": *Incompleat*, 22

"The Weavers . . . there": Dunway, 161

The Weavers rarely performed: Willens, 123

"looked . . . moose": Judy Freeman, interview

"He wasn't . . . him": Dunway, 89

41 "He genuinely . . . living it": Van Ronk, 67–69

"songs and . . . hype": Dunway, 167

"The legend holds . . . sleep": Dunway, 166

"Goodnight, Irene": Wilkinson, 71

42   "The summer . . . someplace": Willens, 126

43   Weaver performances: Dunway, 175–77

Toshi's role with the Weavers: Dunway, xx, 13, 164, 171, 182–83

6. Under Suspicion

45   *"And for . . . rose"*: *Flowers*, 129

"extremely . . . appearance": Dunway, 95

Pete Seeger and the Communist Party: Rosenthal, 100;
     Dunway, 175–77; Willens, 126; Seeger, interview with the author,
     February 18, 2009

45   "I should . . . going on": Wilkinson, 116

46   " 'communist' with a small *c* ": Seeger, interview with the author,
     February 18, 2009

Red Channels: Dunway, 175–77; Wilkinson, 72

48   Harvey Matusow: Rosenthal, 95

48-49   "Jack . . . clean": Lichtman and Cohen, *Deadly Farce*, 58

49   Matusow's testimony: Willens, 135

49-50   "We have . . . we do": Rosenthal, 94

50   "Did you . . . Communist": Van Ronk, 39

Daffy's Bar and Grill: Dunway, 156

the Weavers: Dunway, 188; Willens, 150

Seeger's property: Dunway, 220

"Toshi . . . scared": Rosenthal, 53

50-51   red diaper babies: Kaplan and Shapiro, *Red Diapers*

52   HUAC's questioning of American citizens: Dunway, 199

"felt . . . know": Willens, 151

7. Fighting Back

53   Pete and the Weavers: Willens, 180–84

54-55   Playing on radio: Dunway, 191

55   *Sing Out!*: *Incompleat*, 154–55; *Flowers*, 201

57   "Are you . . . for you": Dunway, 198

       "Some good . . . singing": Dunway, 206

60   "No blacklisted . . . spy": Willens, 152

       First Amendment rights: Rosenthal, 105

       The Hollywood Ten: Wilkinson, 75

60-61   "I am . . . sir": HUAC, August 18, 1955

61   Harold Leventhal: Willens, 164

       Pete writing songs: Dunway, 227, 230

63   Pete's inspiring young singers: Dunway, 240; Wilkinson, 85

       Pete's jail time and dismissed indictment: Dunway, 253, 259

       "When . . . doing it": Dunway, 254

8. Joining Forces

66   "We Shall Overcome": Dunway, 175, 275

       World tour: *Incompleat*, 530

67   "Kids . . . will come,": *Pete Seeger: Live in Australia 1963*

68   Meridian, Mississippi.: Willens, 214–15

       "What . . . fortunes": *Incompleat*, 260; Rosenthal, 120

       "There's nothing . . . cheers": *Flowers,* 147

       "In the . . . awe": Judy Freeman, interview

69   Judy Collins: Sandel, "Sweet Judy Blue Eyes"

70   "One moment . . . cut": *Flowers,* 149; Dunway, 328, 335

70-72   the March on Washington and attendant quotes: *Flowers,* 156–57

72 "The sight . . . make it": Rosenthal, 134–35

9. *Singing Together to Save Our Planet*

74 Pete Seeger and his community: Wilkinson, 98

"Sailing on . . . past me": *Flowers,* 201

Vic Schwartz: *Flowers,* 205

Fundraiser for Clearwater: Dunway, 357

75 *Clearwater*: Wilkinson, 104

"The price . . . getting it": Dunway, 361

"What can . . . river": Dunway, 290

76 "A few . . . ever has": Clearwater

76-77 Club activities: Seeger, interview with the author, February 18, 2009

77 Children on the *Clearwater*: Clearwater

77-80 Pete Seeger on environmental issues: Horrigan, "Hudson Confidential"; Seeger, interview with the author, February 18, 2009

80 "A farmer . . . butter": *Incompleat,* 307

10. *Pete Seeger's Legacy*

81 "Here is . . . music": Keyes, "Morning Edition"

82 "Everyone's . . . moving": Keyes, "Morning Edition"

83 Five million people: Dunway, xvii

84 Occupy Wall Street: Talbott, "Pete Seeger Enters 9th Decade as an Activist"

84 Pete and his children and grandchildren: Rosenthal, 295

"It's been . . . alone": Wilkinson, 106

85 "Nobody . . . I can": Dunway, 414

BIBLIOGRAPHY

Books and Articles

Dunway, David King. *How Can I Keep from Singing? The Ballad of Pete Seeger.* New York: Villard Books, 2008.

Horrigan, Jeremiah. "Hudson Confidential: Seeger Wants Caulk Guns Loaded and Locked." *Hudson Times Herald Record,* January 21, 2009.

Kaplan, Judy, and Linn Shapiro, eds. *Red Diapers: Growing Up in the Communist Left.* Urbana: University of Illinois Press, 1998.

Lichtman, Robert M., and Ronald D. Cohen. *Deadly Farce: Harvey Matusow and the Informer System in the McCarthy Era.* Urbana: University of Illinois Press, 2004.

Matusow, Harvey. *False Witness.* New York: Cameron & Kahn, 1955.

Moroney, Tom. "Facebook's Zuckerberg Becomes Latest Harvard Dropout to Drop In." *Bloomberg,* November 8, 2011.

Rosenthal, Rob, and Sam Rosenthal. *Pete Seeger: His Life in His Own Words.* Boulder, Colo.: Paradigm Publishers, 2012.

Sandel, Adam. "Sweet Judy Blue Eyes." *Bay Area Reporter,* September 15, 2011.

Seeger, Pete. *Abiyoyo: Based on a South African Lullaby and Folk Story.* Illustrated by Michael Hays. New York: Macmillan, 1986.

———. *The Incompleat Folksinger.* New York: Simon & Schuster, 1972.

———. *Where Have All the Flowers Gone: A Singalong Memoir.* New York: W. W. Norton, 2009.

Silvey, Anita. *Everything I Need to Know I Learned from a Children's Book: Life Lessons from Notable People from All Walks of Life.* New York: Roaring Brook Press, 2009.

Talbott, Chris. "Pete Seeger Enters 9th Decade as an Activist." *AP Newswire,* October 24, 2011.

Twain, Mark. "Enthusiastic Eloquence." *San Francisco Dramatic Chronicle,* June 23, 1865.

Van Ronk, Dave. *The Mayor of MacDougal Street: A Memoir.* Cambridge, Mass.: Da Capo Press, 2005.

Wilkinson, Alan. "The Protest Singer." *The New Yorker,* April 17, 2006.

———. *The Protest Singer: An Intimate Portrait of Pete Seeger.* New York: Vintage Books, 2009.

Willens, Doris. *Lonesome Traveler: The Life of Lee Hays.* Lincoln: University of Nebraska, 1994.

"Woody Guthrie's New Year's Resolutions from 1942." *American Songwriter* magazine, November/December 2011.

Other Media

Clearwater Concert, The. Pete Seeger's 90th Birthday Celebration from Madison Square Garden. DVD. Hudson River Sloop Clearwater, 2009.

Deitch, Gene. "The 65 Greats behind the Scenes." www.genedeitchcredits.com.

Freeman, Judy. Interview with the author, February 13, 2012.

From the Blue Ridge Mountains: Give me the Banjo. PBS Arts, November 4, 2011.

HUAC. August 18, 1955. www.peteseeger.net/HUAC.htm.

Keyes, Allison. *NPR's Morning Edition,* January 18, 2009.

Lomax the Songhunter. DVD. Directed by Rogier Kappers. MM Film, 2004.

Northlands Poster Collective, Minneapolis, Minnesota.

Pete Seeger: Live in Australia 1963. DVD. Acorn Media, 2009.

Seeger, Pete. *Pete Remembers Woody.* CD set. Appleseed, 2012.

———. Interview with the author; December 26, 2008, February 18, 2009.

PHOTO CREDITS

ACKNOWLEDGMENTS

Since *Let Your Voice Be Heard* took eight years to complete, I owe a lot of people thanks along the way. Dinah Stevenson of Clarion suggested to me writing a book about the Weavers, which turned into this biography of Pete Seeger. Vicki Palmquist and Leda Schubert provided valuable Pete Seeger resources in the research process. Judy Freeman shared insights about Pete's power as a performer. Laura Vaccaro Seeger and her wonderful husband Chris introduced me to Pete, and I am so grateful for their continued encouragement. Pete Seeger himself gave me hours of his time for interviews. His generosity of spirit, his passion, and the sound of his voice will be with me forever.

I was fortunate to have one of the best nonfiction copyeditors I have ever encountered in Renée Cafiero. All errors are mine, but she did everything possible to keep me from making them. And Lisa Vega provided a sprightly and attractive design. I was raised in publishing on the Century Schoolbook font, but she made me a convert to Freight Text.

Doe Coover, best of all agents, helped me move through the obstacles and stay on track. Frances Kennedy, Doe's reliable sidekick, provided immense help in securing final permissions for some of the photographs. For all my friends and colleagues who have listened to me discuss Pete Seeger's life and my writer's angst—without you, this book would not exist.

INDEX

Note: Page references in *italics* indicate photo captions.

Abernathy, Ralph, *65*
"Abiyoyo," 57
Almanac Singers, 27, 28, 30–32, 45
American Artists School, 20
Archive of American Folk Song, 20, 22
Avon Old Farms, 12–16, *13*

Baez, Joan, 62, 69, 77
banjo, 13–14, *14, 15*
Beacon Sloop Club, 76–77
Belafonte, Harry, 82

Cahill-Jackson, Kitama, 84
caulk guns, 77–80
Chapman, John, 56
civil rights movement, 64–68, 72
Clearwater (sloop), 74–75, *76, 77*
Collins, Judy, 69
communism, 45–52
Communist Party of America, 45, 50–51
conscientious objector (CO), 5–6
Crawford, Ruth, 12
Cunningham, Sis, 28

Dalton School, 20
Decca Records, 41, 49–50

Deitch, Gene, 38

environmental activism, 73–80

False Witness (Matusow), 49, *49*
Federal Bureau of Investigation (FBI), 45–52
Fifth Amendment, 60
First Amendment, 60
folk music
    in Appalachia, 6
    cataloging of, 20–21, 22
    emotions conveyed in, 15
    expert opinions about, 16

General Electric, 75–76
Gilbert, Ronnie, 39, *39*
"Goodnight, Irene," 41–42, *42*
Guard, Dave, 62
Guthrie, Arlo, 41, 63, 77, 84
Guthrie, Woody, 22–24, *23,* 25–26, 28, 34

Harris, Julie, 82
Harvard University, 16, 45
Hawes, Bess Lomax, 28
Hawes, Pete, 27
Hays, Lee, 27, 32, 38–39, *39,* 48
Hellerman, Fred, 39, *39*
Hollywood Ten, 60
hootenannies, 32

Hoover, J. Edgar, 45, *46*
Horton, Charis, *65*
House Un-American Activities Committee
    (HUAC), 48, 52, 57–61
Hudson River cleanup, 73–77
Hudson River sloop, 74–75, *76*, 77

Japanese American citizens, 33
Jenkins, Gordon, 41
journalism, 15, 18

King, Martin Luther, Jr., 64, *65*, 66, 68
Kingston Trio, 62, 69
Korean War, 46

labor movement, 4–5, 27–31
Lampell, Millard, 27, 28, 40
Ledbetter, Huddie ("Lead Belly"), 21, *21–22*
Ledbetter, Martha, *21*
Lennon, John, 71
Leopold, Aldo, 77
Leventhal, Harold, 61, 66
Library of Congress, 20, 22
The Lion King, 41
Lomax, Alan, 19–22, *20*, 40

Matusow, Harvey, 48–49, 52
McCarthy, Joseph, 48, 57
McGhee, Brownie, 32
Mellencamp, John, 63, 77
Mississippi Summer Project, 67–68
music career
    Almanac Singers, 27, 30–32, 45
    during FBI investigations, 48–50
    learning to perform, 25–26
    mentors, 19–24
    solo performances, 53–57

    the Weavers, 39–44, 48, 49–50, 53
    world tour, 66–67

National Labor Relations Act, 29
Native Americans, 10–11
New York City, in 1940s, 27
Nobel Peace Prize, 83

Obama, Barack, 81
Occupy Wall Street, 83–84
Ono, Yoko, 70
Oriental Exclusion Act, 33

painting, 18–19
Parks, Rosa, *65*
PCBs, 75–76
Pearl Harbor, 33
People's Songs (union), 36
Peter, Paul, and Mary, 69

Red Channels, 46–47, *47*
red diaper babies, 50–51
Robeson, Paul, 1
Rock and Roll Hall of Fame, 83
Roosevelt, Eleanor, *31*
Roosevelt, Franklin D., 33
Ross, Paul, *58*

sailing, 74
Sandburg, Carl, 40
Schwartz, Vic, 74
Seeger, Alan, 5–6
Seeger, Charles, Jr., 4–8, *5, 7, 8*, 12
Seeger, Constance, 4, *7*, 7–8, *8*
Seeger, Danny, 36, 43, 50, *51*
Seeger, Elizabeth, 20
Seeger, John, *7, 8*

Seeger, Mika, 36, 43, 50, *51*
Seeger, Peggy, 38
Seeger, Pete. *See also* music career
    ancestors, 3–4
    antiwar protests, 69–72
    artistic talents, 18–19
    awards and accolades, 83
    Beacon, NY home, 37–38, 74
    birth and childhood, 6–12
    career exploration, 18–19
    character, 25
    civil rights work, 64–68
    college years, 16, 45
    death, 83
    documentary about, 84
    environmental activism, 73–80
    half brothers and sisters, 12
    HUAC testimony, 57–61
    indictment dismissed, 63
    investigated by FBI, 45–52
    legacy, 81–85
    marriage, 34
    ninetieth birthday concert, 77, 79
    photos of, *7, 8, 28, 31, 35, 39, 51, 54, 55, 59, 62, 65, 67, 71, 79, 82*
    private school years, 12–16
    road trip with Woody Guthrie, 25–26
    sentenced for contempt of Congress, 63
    singing style, 25
    in World War II, 34–36
Seeger, Tao Rodriguez, 84
Seeger, Tinya, 50, *51*
Seeger, Toshi Ohta, 32–34, 36, 43, 44, 50, *51*, 83
Seton, Ernest Thompson, 10, *11*, 80
Sing Out! publication, 55–56, *56*
Smothers, Tommy, 70

The Smothers Brothers Comedy Hour, 70
Soviet Union, 46
Springsteen, Bruce, 63, 77, 81
Stern, Arthur, 28

Terry, Sonny, 32
The Today Show, 75
"Turn, Turn, Turn," 69

ukulele, 12–13
unions, labor, 27–31

Vietnam War, 64, 69–72

"Waist Deep in the Big Muddy," 69, 70
Weavers, the, 39, *39*–44, 48, 49–50, 53
"We Shall Overcome," 66, 84
"Where Have All the Flowers Gone?," 69
World War I, 5
World War II, 33–36